THE PERFECT — THANKSGIVING BOOK

THE PERFECT
THANKSGIVING BOOK

LORENZ BOOKS
NEW YORK · LONDON · SYDNEY · BATH

First published by Lorenz Books in 1995

© 1995 Anness Publishing Limited

Lorenz Books is an imprint of
Anness Publishing Limited
Boundary Row Studios
1 Boundary Row
London SE1 8HP

This edition distributed in Canada by
Raincoast Books Distribution Limited.

ISBN 1 85967 121 7

Publisher: Joanna Lorenz
Senior Cookery Editor: Linda Fraser
Designer: Lisa Tai
Photographers: Karl Adamson, Amanda Heywood, Nelson Hargreaves,
Michael Michaels, James Duncan and Michelle Garrett
Recipes: Laura Washburn, Frances Cleary,
Shirley Gill, Patricia Lousada, Katherine Richmond,
Pamela Westland and Roz Denny
Craft Projects: Terence Moore, Bridget Jones,
Madeleine Brehaut and Pamela Westland

Typeset by MC Typeset Ltd, Rochester, Kent
Printed in Singapore by Star Standard Industries Pte. Ltd.

CONTENTS

THE STORY OF THANKSGIVING

Indian summer soon came in a blaze of glory, and it was time to bring in the crops. All in all, their first harvest was a disappointment. Their twenty acres of corn, thanks to Squanto, had done well enough. But the Pilgrims failed miserably with more familiar crops. Their six or seven acres of English wheat, barley, and peas came to nothing, and Bradford was certainly on safe ground in attributing this either to "ye badnes of ye seed, or latenes of ye season, or both, or some other defecte." Still, it was possible to make a substantial increase in the individual weekly food ration which for months had consisted merely of a peck of meal from the stores brought on the Mayflower. This was now doubled by adding a peck of maize a

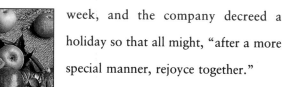

week, and the company decreed a holiday so that all might, "after a more special manner, rejoyce together."

The Pilgrims had other things to be thankful for. They had made peace with the Indians and walked "as peaceably and safely in the woods as in the highways in England." A start had been made in the beaver trade. There had been no sickness for months. Eleven houses now lined the street – seven private dwellings and four buildings for common use. There had been no recurrence of mutiny and dissension. Faced with common dangers, Saints and Strangers had drawn closer together, sinking doctrinal differences for a time. Nothing had disturbed the peace but a duel, the first and last fought in the colony, with Stephen Hopkins' spirited young servants, Edward Dotey and Edward Leister, as principals.

As the day of the harvest festival approached, four men were sent out to shoot waterfowl, returning with enough to supply the company for a week. Massasoit was invited to attend and shortly arrived – with ninety ravenous braves! The strain on the larder was somewhat eased when some of these went out and bagged five deer. Captain Standish staged a military review, there were games of skill and chance, and for three days the Pilgrims and their guests gorged themselves on venison, roast duck, roast goose, clams and other shellfish, succulent eels, white bread, corn bread, leeks and watercress and other "sallet herbes," with wild plums and dried berries as dessert – all washed down with wine, made of the wild grape, both white and red, which the Pilgrims praised as "very sweete & strong." At this first Thanksgiving feast in New England the company may have enjoyed, though there is no mention of it in the record, some of the long-legged "Turkies" whose speed of foot in the woods constantly amazed the Pilgrims. And there were cranberries by the bushel in neighboring bogs. It is very doubtful, however, if the Pilgrims had yet contrived a happy use for them. Nor was the table graced with a later and even more felicitous invention – pumpkin pie.

The celebration was a great success, warmly satisfying to body and soul alike, and the Pilgrims held another the next year, repeating it more or less regularly for generations. In time it became traditional throughout New England to enjoy the harvest feast with Pilgrim trimmings, a tradition carried to other parts of the country as restless Yankees moved westward. But it remained a regional or local holiday until 1863 when President Lincoln, in the midst of the Civil War, proclaimed the first national Thanksgiving, setting aside the last Thursday in November for the purpose, disregarding the centuries-old Pilgrim custom of holding it somewhat earlier, usually in October as on this first occasion.

From *Saints and Strangers* by George F. Willison

SETTING UP

Most everyone would agree that the finest moment of Thanksgiving is just before sitting down; when everyone looks at the table, gleaming with candlelight, glowing with color and smelling like heaven on earth. Creating a beautiful tablescape does not have to be intricate and time-consuming but it can make the difference between an ordinary meal and a memorable feast – stunning arrangements can be made in minutes and are well worth the minimal effort. Fruits, nuts, berries, bittersweet and other vines, candles, a bit of gold paint and some pine cones are all you need to make magic.

Anna

CANDLEBRIGHT

~

Pumpkin-shaped gourds are a logical choice for candleholders at Thanksgiving.

Arrange them in a cluster on the table or on a prominent sideboard if you don't have room.

YOU WILL NEED
pumpkin-shaped gourds
apple corer, sharp knife,
or florist's adhesive clay
 (see below)
candles

If you have more gourds than you will need for candleholders, select those with the most attractive curved stalks and set them aside. Break off the stalks from the others and, if the gourd is soft enough, gouge out a shallow hole wide enough to hold a candle. If the gourd is too hard – and dried ones may well be – fix the candles securely in the indentation with florist's adhesive clay. If candles are fixed in this way, take extra care when they are lighted. Do not leave them unattended with boisterous youngsters or animals.

AUTUMN CANDLE POTS

These cheerful candleholders take minutes to assemble and can be used over and over again.
Use your imagination when choosing materials: along with nuts and pine cones, bits of twig,
or interesting seed pods can add wonderful texture.

YOU WILL NEED
small terracotta pots
reindeer moss
nuts in their shells:
  hazelnuts, almonds,
  walnuts, brazil nuts
pine cones
seed pods and twigs
  (optional)
glue or glue gun

Fill each pot with reindeer moss piling up an inch or so over the edge of the pot. This will form a base for the candle and a pillow for the ring of nuts to sit on. Begin to build a broad collar of nuts and pine cones around the rim of the pot, making sure to leave enough space in the center for the candle. When this is complete, press bits of moss into any obvious chinks and insert the candle into the center.

Caution: Do not leave burning candles unattended.

HARVEST BASKET

For this forest-filled basket, try to incorporate items that you have gleaned yourself from a country walk – leaves, seed pods, acorns, nuts, moss, lichens – for a truly natural display.

YOU WILL NEED
good-sized round basket
hay collar
stub (floral) wires
equal quantities of mixed
*   nuts such as walnuts,*
*   brazil nuts, hazelnuts*

fir cones
bunches of small twigs
moss
cutters
glue gun

Make a hay collar about ¾ in in diameter and long enough to fit inside the top edge of the basket (left). Fix in place with stub (floral) wires, each about 1 in apart: thread the wire through the basket, bring the two ends up and round the hay collar, twist them together as tightly as possible and tuck the loose ends into the collar.

Using the glue gun (right), start adding the ingredients to the collar in small groups of each variety.

When you have added most of the items, wire up small bunches of twigs and glue into place. Cover with smaller nuts, and fill in any gaps with moss.

The finished woodland Harvest Basket looks better the more haphazard and uneven it is. It can either be left empty, or you could add some simple flowers – wire miniature red roses into 2–3 small bunches, for instance, and place them in the center of the basket. Or, as an alternative to flowers you could add a good woodland-mix pot pourri.

If you have a fairly open-weave basket, make sure that you line the inside with a sheet of tissue paper first to prevent any pot pourri from falling through.

Do not worry if the material is a little damp, as the display will soon dry out. For a long-lasting piece of work, you may wish to glaze the finished arrangement with florist's clear sealer.

WHEAT NAPKIN RING

This simple napkin ring adds a rustic charm to Thanksgiving, harvest suppers
or any mealtime occasion when the nights are drawing in.

YOU WILL NEED
(for each ring)
three small dried leaves
fine florist's wire
paper varnish and
brush

three ears of wheat with
10 in stems attached
three 10 in lengths of
stalk without heads
hot water
ribbon

headless stalks. Plait (braid) the wheat stalks together
as evenly as possible (above). Twist the plait into a ring
(below left) and wire in place. Neaten the end. Tie a
ribbon bow below the leaves and wheat ears (below
right) to conceal the join and give a festive finish to the
napkin ring.

Wire the leaf stems, then paint with paper
varnish (above left). Allow to dry.

Soak the wheat stalks for about 30 minutes in very
hot water to soften them. Drain and blot dry. Very
gently insert a length of florist's wire into each stalk,
leaving a little wire protruding at
the ends of the stalks.

Attach a leaf to the base of each wheat
ear (above right), then wire in one of the

CANDLE NAPKIN

~

This festive fold is the perfect holiday touch. Green or red napkins are particularly cheerful
but you could use any color to suit your table color scheme.

YOU WILL NEED
red or green
  square napkins

Starting with the corners of the open napkin top
and bottom in the form of a diamond, fold the
corner nearest to you to meet the top point. Next fold
the bottom edge up a short way to form a narrow hem.

Hold the hem firmly, and carefully turn over the
napkin so that the long folded edge is to your right.
Then roll up the napkin (below left) from the bottom
point and stopping short of the small top tail.

Turn the candle round so that the tail now faces you
and tuck the tail into the band to secure the roll.

Tuck the top loose point into the roll and form a
flame shape with the second point (below right).

STANDING PLACE CARDS

~

Place cards are always laid at Thanksgiving. There is something ordered and reassuring
about knowing your place at the table, and the cards can be reused year after year.

YOU WILL NEED
cardboard
paper
pencil
sticky tape
craft knife

stencil or sheet of acetate
waterproof black felt-tip
 pen
gold paint
stencil brush
thin colored ribbon

Cut a strip of card-board measuring
6 × 3 inches. Mark a
fold across the center of
the card and a 1 inch
fold at each end of the
strip. Lightly score the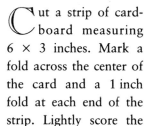
folds with a craft knife (right), but be careful not to
cut completely through the card.

If you are making your own stencil, draw your
design onto a sheet of paper. Place the sheet of acetate
on top and tape in position to hold the sheet in place.
Transfer the design to the acetate using the felt-tip pen.
Cut around the outline of the design using the craft
knife. Lightly load the brush with gold paint – too
much paint will spoil the print. Holding the stencil
firmly in position, press the brush over the pattern in
the stencil keeping the brush vertical (above right).

To attach the ribbon, cut two small slits in the card.
Thread the ribbon through and tie into a bow (above
right). Trim the ends of the ribbon.

TO BEGIN

It is generally a good idea to keep the hors d'oeuvres and appetizers light and easy on Thanksgiving Day, as you don't want your guests to fill up before they sit down to the feast. However, you will need to serve something as the mouthwatering smells waft out of the kitchen. An interesting array of crudites with a selection of simple dips, some oysters on the half shell or shrimp cocktail, a bowl of different colored olives, with or without feta cheese, are some of the no-fuss nibbles you could offer. Accompany them with a festive champagne cocktail or an equally delicous sparkling cider alternative.

STRAWBERRY AND MINT CHAMPAGNE

This is a simple concoction that makes a bottle of champagne go a lot further.
It tastes as festive as it looks.

SERVES 4–6
1 pound strawberries
6–8 fresh mint leaves

1 bottle champagne or
sparkling white wine

Purée the strawberries and mint leaves in a food processor (above left).
Strain through a fine sieve into a bowl (above right). Half fill a glass with the mixture and top up with champagne. Decorate with a sprig of mint.

COOK'S TIP
If strawberries are unavailable you can substitute almost any fresh or frozen fruit: blueberries, raspberries, mango and peach are just a few of the elegant and colorful possibilities you could choose.

ORCHARD FIZZ

Sparkling apple juice has enough of the rising-bubbles factor to qualify as a delicious non-alcoholic Thanksgiving cocktail. Decorate with thinly sliced limes and kiwi fruit.

MAKES 10 GLASSES
10 *sugar cubes*
2 *lemons, thinly sliced*
¾ *cup lime juice*
4⅓ *cups sparkling apple juice*

1 *cup club soda or seltzer*
2 *limes, thinly sliced*
2 *kiwi fruits, peeled and thinly sliced*
mint sprigs

Rub the sugar cubes over the lemons to remove the zest. Place one in each glass. Squeeze the lemons and put the juice in a chilled pitcher with the lime and apple juice and soda. Mix together and float the fruit slices and mint on top. Serve in chilled glasses.

HERB GOAT CHEESE DIP

This light dip will leave plenty of room for the feast to come. Use a colorful array of vegetables for dunking: along with standards such as carrots, celery and cherry tomatoes add some raw artichoke leaves, peeled scallions and apple slices for the more adventurous.

MAKES ABOUT 2 CUPS
10 ounces soft mild
  goat cheese
½ cup light cream or half
  and half
2 teaspoons fresh lemon
  juice
1 tablespoon chopped
  fresh chives

1 tablespoon chopped
  fresh parsley
2 tablespoons chopped
  fresh basil
black pepper
raw or briefly cooked
  cold vegetables, potato
  chips, or crackers,
  for serving

In a food processor or blender, combine the goat cheese and cream and process to blend. Add the lemon juice and process until thoroughly mixed and smooth (below left).

Scrape into a bowl. Stir in the chives, parsley, basil, and pepper to taste (left). Chill to set slightly, then serve cold, as a dip for prepared vegetables, potato chips, or crackers.

SALMON RILLETTES

A light smoked fish appetizer is perfect hors d'oeuvre fare on Thanksgiving.
These rillettes can be made up to two days ahead – a boon for busy cooks.

SERVES 6

12 ounces salmon fillets
¾ cup butter, softened
1 celery stalk, finely
   chopped
1 leek, white part only,
   finely chopped
1 bay leaf

⅔ cup dry white wine
4 ounces smoked salmon
   trimmings
generous pinch of ground
   mace
4 tablespoons ricotta
salt and black pepper
salad leaves, to serve

Lightly season the salmon. Melt 2 tablespoons of the butter in a medium sauté pan. Add the celery and leek and cook for about 5 minutes. Add the salmon and bay leaf and pour over the wine. Cover and cook for about 15 minutes until the fish is tender.

Strain the cooking liquid into a pan and boil until reduced to about 2 tablespoons. Cool. Meanwhile, melt 4 tablespoons of the remaining butter and gently cook the smoked salmon until it turns pale pink. Leave to cool.

Remove the skin and any bones from the salmon fillets. Flake the flesh into a bowl and add the reduced, cooled cooking liquid.

Beat in the remaining butter, the mace and ricotta. Break up the smoked salmon and fold into the mixture with the pan juices. Taste and adjust the seasoning.

Spoon the salmon mixture into a dish or terrine and smooth the top level. Cover and chill. To serve, shape the mixture into quenelles using two dessert spoons and arrange on salad leaves with wheat crackers.

SHRIMP AND CORN BISQUE

This light, creamy soup has a beautiful pale yellow and pink color and an irresistible taste,
ideal to begin a Thanksgiving meal.

SERVES 4

2 tablespoons olive oil

1 onion, minced

4 tablespoons butter
   or margarine

¼ cup flour

3 cups fish or chicken
   stock, or clam juice

1 cup milk

1 cup peeled cooked

small shrimp, deveined
   if necessary

1½ cups corn kernels
   (fresh, frozen, or
   canned)

½ teaspoon minced fresh
   dill or thyme

salt

hot pepper sauce

½ cup light cream

Heat the olive oil in a large heavy saucepan. Add the onion and cook over low heat for about 8–10 minutes until softened.

Meanwhile, melt the butter or margarine in a medium-size saucepan. Add the flour and stir with a wire whisk until blended. Cook for 1–2 minutes. Pour in the stock and milk and stir to blend. Bring to a boil over medium heat and cook for 5–8 minutes, stirring.

Cut each shrimp into 2 or 3 pieces and add to the onion with the corn and herb. Cook for 2–3 minutes,

stirring occasionally. Remove from the heat.

Add the sauce mixture to the shrimp and corn mixture and mix well. Remove 3 cups of the soup and purée in a blender or food processor. Return it to the rest of the soup in the pan and stir well. Season with salt and hot pepper sauce to taste.

Add the cream and stir to blend. Heat the soup almost to boiling point, stirring frequently. Serve hot.

CARROT AND CORIANDER SOUP

Use a good homemade stock for this soup, if possible — it adds a far greater depth of flavor than stock made from cubes.

SERVES 4
4 tablespoons butter
3 leeks, sliced
1 pound carrots, peeled and sliced
1 tablespoon ground coriander
5 cups light chicken stock
2/3 cup strained plain yogurt
salt and black pepper
2–3 tablespoons chopped cilantro, to garnish

Melt the butter in a large pan. Add the leeks and carrots and stir well, coating the vegetables with the butter. Cover and cook for about 10 minutes, until the vegetables are beginning to soften but not color.

Stir in the ground coriander and cook for about 1 minute. Pour in the stock (below left) and add seasoning. Bring to a boil, cover and simmer for 20 minutes, until the leeks and carrots are tender.

Leave to cool slightly, then purée in a blender until smooth. Return the soup to the pan and add about 2 tablespoons of the yogurt (left), taste the soup and adjust the seasoning. Reheat gently but do not boil.

Ladle the soup into bowls and put a spoonful of the remaining yogurt in the center of each. Scatter over the cilantro and serve immediately.

SPICED PARSNIP SOUP

This pale creamy-textured soup is given a special touch with an aromatic,
spiced garlic and mustard seed garnish.

SERVES 4–6

3 tablespoons butter
1 onion, chopped
1½ pounds parsnips,
    diced
1 teaspoon ground
    coriander
½ teaspoon ground
    cumin
½ teaspoon ground
    turmeric
¼ teaspoon chili powder
5 cups chicken stock
⅔ cup light cream
1 tablespoon sunflower
    oil
1 garlic clove, cut into
    julienne strips
2 teaspoons yellow
    mustard seeds
salt and black pepper

Cool slightly, then
purée in a blender until
smooth. Return the soup
to the pan (right), add
the cream and heat gently
over a low heat.

Heat the oil in a small
pan, add the julienne
strips of garlic and yellow
mustard seeds (below) and fry quickly until the garlic
begins to brown and the mustard seeds start to pop
and splutter. Remove the pan from the heat.

Ladle the soup into warmed soup bowls and pour a
little of the hot spice mixture over each. Serve at once.

M̲elt the butter in a
large pan, add the
onion and parsnips and
fry gently for about 3
minutes until beginning
to soften but not brown.

Stir in the spices (right)
and cook for 1 minute.

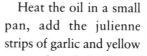

Add the stock, season to taste with
salt and pepper and bring to a
boil, then reduce the heat. Cover
and simmer for about 45 minutes,
until the parsnips are tender.

THE MAIN EVENT

Turkey, the joyous discovery of New World settlers in the seventeenth century, has since gained in popularity across the Western world as the prime festive offering. In the United States turkey is devoured with equal relish at Thanksgiving and then, scarcely a month later, on Christmas Day. In Britain this plump bird has replaced goose as the most popular Christmas Day fare; and in the rest of Europe, turkey is gaining ground. In Greece, for example, it now takes pride of place over traditional roast pork, and even in Germany it now frequently displaces goose on the Christmas table.

ROAST TURKEY AND CHESTNUT STUFFING

The centerpiece of the Thanksgiving feast is a juicy roast turkey served with a
rich tangy stuffing and delicious spicy gravy.

SERVES 10–12
1 × 10 pound oven-ready
  turkey
½ cup butter, softened
½ lemon
salt and pepper

For the gravy
giblets and neck from the
  bird, if available
4 cloves
1 onion, skinned and
  quartered
2 stalks celery, sliced
1 carrot, sliced
2½ cups water
1 tablespoon flour
3 tablespoons dry white
  wine

For the stuffing
3 tablespoons butter
1 large onion, chopped
1 lb can unsweetened
  chestnut purée
1 cup fresh white bread
  crumbs
3 tablespoons orange
  juice
grated nutmeg
½ teaspoon sugar
salt and black pepper

Remove from the heat and mix with the chestnut
purée, bread crumbs, orange juice, nutmeg and sugar.

Season with salt and pepper. Allow to cool, and use
to pack one end of the turkey.

Ease the skin away from the breast meat and rub in
the softened butter (above left). Rub the skin with the
lemon and season with salt and pepper. Place the bird
breast-side up on a wire rack in a roasting pan and
cover it loosely with foil. Do not wrap tightly or the
bird will steam rather than roast in the oven.

Place the pan in the oven. After 20 minutes, reduce
the heat to 350°F and continue cooking for a further
3½ hours, basting the turkey with the fat and pan
juices every 20 or 25 minutes.

Remove the foil, baste the turkey again (above right)
and increase the oven temperature to 400°F. Continue
cooking the bird, uncovered, to brown the skin for a

Remove the turkey from the refrigerator at least 3
hours before cooking. Heat the oven to 425°F.
Wipe the turkey inside and out with a damp cloth and
dry it with paper towels. For the stuffing, heat the
butter in a pan and fry the onion for about 3 minutes.

further 30 minutes, or until the meat is well cooked. To test that the turkey is ready to serve, insert a fine skewer into the thickest part of the legs. The juices that run out should be clear and show no traces of pink. If the juices are still pink, return the turkey to the oven and cook for a further 20 minutes, then test again.

To make the gravy, place the giblets and neck in a pan. Stick the cloves into the onion and add to the pan with the celery and carrot. Pour on the water. Slowly bring to a boil and skim off the foam that rises to the surface. Cover the pan and simmer for 1 hour.

When the turkey is cooked, transfer it to a warmed serving plate, cover it loosely with foil and keep it warm until ready to serve.

Pour off the fat from the turkey pan, reserving the juices. Stir in the flour over a low heat until it forms a roux. Strain the stock from the saucepan and gradually stir it into the roux. Add the wine and stir until the gravy thickens and is smooth and glossy. Season to taste with salt and pepper. Serve hot.

CORNISH GAME HENS WITH CRANBERRY SAUCE

~

If you are having a small gathering these little individual birds are a perfect solution
and will be a delightful surprise for your guests.

SERVES 4

4 *Cornish game hens,*
  with giblets, each about
  1 pound
3 *tablespoons butter*
  or margarine

salt and pepper
1 *onion, quartered*
¼ *cup port wine*
⅔ *cup chicken stock*
2 *tablespoons honey*
1½ *cups fresh cranberries*

Preheat the oven to 450°F. Rub the hens on all sides with 2 tablespoons of the butter or margarine. Arrange them, on their sides, in a roasting pan in which they will fit comfortably. Sprinkle with salt and pepper. Add the onion quarters. Chop the gizzards and livers and arrange around the hens.

Roast 20 minutes, basting often with the melted fat in the pan. Turn the hens onto their other sides and roast 20 minutes longer, basting often. Turn the hens breast up and continue roasting until they are cooked through, about 15 minutes. Transfer the hens to a warmed serving dish. Cover with foil and set aside.

Skim any fat off the juices in the roasting pan. Put the pan on top of the stove and bring the juices to a boil. Add the port wine and bring back to a boil, stirring well to dislodge any particles attached to the bottom of the pan.

Strain into a saucepan. Add the stock, bring to a boil, and reduce by half. Stir in the honey and cranberries. Simmer until the berries pop, about 3 minutes. Remove the pan from the heat and swirl in the remaining butter or margarine. Season to taste. Pour into a sauceboat and serve with the hens.

CRANBERRY AND PORT SAUCE
WITH LEMON THYME

This tart/sweet sauce makes a delicious change from the traditional cranberry.
If you can't find lemon thyme plain thyme works equally well.

MAKES ABOUT 2½ CUPS
4 tablespoons port wine
4 tablespoons orange
  juice
½ cup sugar

8 ounces fresh
  cranberries, picked over
1 tablespoon finely grated
  orange rind
1 tablespoon very finely
  chopped lemon thyme

Pour the port wine and orange juice into a saucepan and add the sugar (below left). Place the pan over a low heat and stir to dissolve the sugar.

Transfer the mixture to a larger pan. Increase the heat a little and add the cranberries. Bring the mixture to a boil and simmer for 5 minutes, stirring occasionally, until the cranberries are just tender and the skins begin to burst.

Remove the pan from the heat and carefully mix in the orange rind and lemon thyme (left). Serve hot with the roast turkey as an alternative to (or accompanying) the gravy.

BAKED PUMPKIN

~

Serving this hearty dish in a pumpkin shell is both efficient and visually stunning.
The vegetarians at your table will bless you for including it on the menu.

SERVES 4
1 × 4 pound pumpkin
1 onion, sliced
1 inch cube fresh ginger
   root
3 tablespoons extra virgin
   olive oil
1 zucchini, sliced
4 ounces sliced
   mushrooms

1 × 14 ounce can
   chopped tomatoes
1 cup pasta shells
2 cups stock
salt and pepper
4 tablespoons ricotta
2 tablespoons fresh basil,
   chopped

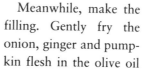

Bake the pumpkin with its lid on for 45 minutes to one hour until the inside begins to soften.

Meanwhile, make the filling. Gently fry the onion, ginger and pumpkin flesh in the olive oil for about 10 minutes, stirring occasionally (above).

Add the zucchini and mushrooms and cook for a further 3 minutes, then stir in the tomatoes, pasta shells and stock. Season well, bring to a boil, then cover and simmer gently for 10 minutes.

Stir the ricotta and chopped basil into the pasta mixture, tossing it together gently, and spoon the mixture into the pumpkin. (It may not be possible to fit  all the filling into the pumpkin shell, so serve the rest separately if this is the case).

Preheat the oven to 350°F. Cut the top off the pumpkin with a large, sharp knife, then scoop out and discard all the seeds (above left).

Using a small, sharp knife and a sturdy tablespoon extract as much of the pumpkin flesh as possible (above right), then chop it into chunks.

Couscous-stuffed Cabbage

This grain and lentil-stuffed cabbage makes a festive side dish or a delightful
alternative entree. It can be made ahead and steamed when required.

SERVES 4

1 medium-size cabbage
1 cup couscous grains
1 onion, chopped
1 small red bell pepper,
  chopped
2 garlic cloves, crushed
2 tablespoons olive oil
1 teaspoon ground
  coriander
1/2 teaspoon ground
  cumin
good pinch ground
  cinnamon

1/2 cup green lentils,
  soaked
2 1/2 cups stock
2 tablespoons tomato
  paste
salt and ground black
  pepper
2 tablespoons fresh
  parsley, chopped
2 tablespoons pine nuts
  or flaked almonds
3 ounces sharp Cheddar
  cheese, grated
1 egg, beaten

Cut the top quarter off the cabbage and remove
any loose outer leaves. Using a small sharp knife,
cut out as much of the middle as you can. Reserve a
few of the larger leaves for later.

Blanch the cabbage in a pan of boiling water for 5
minutes, then drain it well, upside down.

Steam the couscous according to the instructions on
the package, until the grains are light and fluffy.

Lightly fry the onion, pepper and garlic in the oil for
5 minutes until soft then stir in the spices and cook for
a further 2 minutes. Add the lentils and pour in the
stock and tomato paste. Bring to a boil, season and
simmer for 25 minutes until the lentils are cooked.

Mix in the couscous, parsley, nuts, cheese and egg.
Open up the cabbage and spoon in the stuffing.

Blanch the leftover outer cabbage leaves, place over
the stuffing, then wrap the whole cabbage in a sheet of
buttered foil. Place in a steamer over simmering water
and cook for about 45 minutes. Remove from the foil
and serve cut into wedges.

BAKED EGGPLANT CASSEROLE

This delicious casserole can be made ahead of time and reheated on Thanksgiving Day.

SERVES 8

2 large eggplants, sliced

6 zucchini, cut in chunks

2/3 cup olive oil, plus
  extra if required

1 1/2 pounds potatoes,
  thinly sliced

2 onions, sliced

3 garlic cloves, crushed

2/3 cup dry white wine

2 × 14 ounce cans
  chopped tomatoes

2 tablespoons tomato
  paste

1 × 15 ounce can green
  lentils

2 teaspoons dried
  oregano

4 tablespoons chopped
  fresh parsley

2 cups feta cheese,
  crumbled

salt and black pepper

For the béchamel sauce

3 tablespoons butter

4 tablespoons flour

2 1/2 cups milk

2 eggs, beaten

4 tablespoons freshly
  grated Parmesan cheese

nutmeg, freshly grated

Salt the eggplants and zucchini in a colander. Leave to drain 30 minutes, rinse and pat dry. Heat the oil in a frying pan and quickly brown the eggplant and zucchini. Remove and drain on paper towel. Brown the potato, remove and pat dry. Add the onion and garlic with a little extra oil and brown. Pour in the wine, cook until reduced then add the tomatoes, paste and lentils and their liquid. Stir in herbs and season. Cover and simmer 15 minutes. In an ovenproof dish, layer the vegetables. Trickle the sauce and feta cheese in between. Top with a layer of eggplant slices. Cover with foil and bake at 375°F for 25 minutes.

For the sauce, put the butter, flour and milk into a pan, bring slowly to a boil, stirring until thick. Season and add the nutmeg. Remove the sauce, cool for 5 minutes then beat in the eggs. Pour over the eggplant and sprinkle with the Parmesan. To finish, return to the oven uncovered and bake for 25–30 minutes until golden and bubbling.

ON THE SIDE

The fleet of serving dishes filled with tasty, brightly colored vegetables is as much a part of the Thanksgiving meal as the turkey. Everyone has his or her favorite, and recipes are passed down from generation to generation though they may be closely guarded secrets within families! When choosing the accompaniments for your turkey or other roast meat keep the different colors as well as the range of flavors of the vegetables in mind: bright green peas, orange sweet potatoes, deep green broccoli and snowy cauliflower are just a few of the autumn's offerings that you should consider including.

PEAR AND PECAN SALAD

Toasted pecans have a special affinity for crisp white pears. Their robust flavors combine especially well with a rich blue cheese dressing and make this a salad to remember.

SERVES 8
1 cup shelled pecans,
  roughly chopped
6 ripe pears
12 ounces young spinach,
  stems removed

heads of 2 escarole or
  Boston lettuce
1 head of radicchio
2 tablespoons blue
  cheese dressing

Place the pecans on a baking sheet and toast them under a moderate broiler to bring out their full flavor (above).

Cut the pears into even slices, leaving the skin intact, and discarding the cores (right).

Wash the salad leaves and spin dry. Add the pears together with the toasted pecans, then toss with the dressing (far right).

PEAS AND LETTUCE

~

Do not discard the tough, outer leaves of lettuce – they are delicious if shredded,
cooked with peas, and flavored with nutmeg.

SERVES 8
12 outer leaves of lettuce,
   e.g. Boston, Romaine
2 small onions or
   shallots, sliced
4 tablespoons butter

or margarine
1 pound fresh or frozen
   peas
fresh nutmeg, grated
salt and ground black
   pepper

Pull off the outer leaves of the lettuce and wash them well. Roughly shred the leaves with your hands (above).

In a saucepan, lightly fry the lettuce and onion or shallot in the butter or margarine for 3 minutes (right).

Add the peas, nutmeg to taste and seasoning. Stir, cover and simmer for about 5 minutes. This dish can be drained or served slightly wet.

GLAZED CARROTS AND SCALLIONS

The tangy sweetness of honey and orange combines with the scallions
to give the baby carrots an oriental flavor.

SERVES 8

1½ pounds baby carrots,
trimmed and peeled
if necessary
2 tablespoons butter or
margarine
3 tablespoons honey

3 tablespoons fresh
orange juice
12 ounces scallions, cut
diagonally into 1-inch
pieces
salt and pepper

Cook the carrots in boiling salted water or steam them until they are just tender, about 10 minutes. Drain if necessary.

In a skillet (above), melt the butter or margarine with the honey and orange juice, stirring until the mixture is smooth and well combined.

Add the carrots and scallions to the skillet (right).

Cook over medium heat, stirring occasionally, until the vegetables are heated through and glazed, about 5 minutes. Season with salt and pepper before serving.

BROCCOLI AND CAULIFLOWER WITH CIDER AND APPLE MINT SAUCE

This cider sauce could be used with other vegetables but it complements
the broccoli and cauliflower beautifully.

SERVES 4
2 large onions, chopped
4 large carrots, chopped
2 large cloves garlic
2 tablespoons dill seeds
8 large sprigs apple mint
4 tablespoons olive oil

4 tablespoons flour
2½ cups cider
2 pounds broccoli florets
2 pounds cauliflower
   florets
4 tablespoons tamari
4 teaspoons mint jelly

Sauté the onions, carrots, garlic, dill seeds and
apple mint leaves in the olive oil until nearly
cooked (above). Stir in the flour and cook for half a
minute or so. Then pour in the cider and simmer gently
until the sauce looks glossy.

Boil the broccoli and cauliflower in separate pots
until just tender.

Pour the sauce into a
food processor and add
the tamari and the mint
jelly (left). Blend until
finely puréed. Pour over
the broccoli and cauli-
flower, and serve.

PERFECT MASHED POTATOES

~

Using olive oil instead of butter makes these mashed potatoes especially light and fluffy.
They are absolutely required at Thanksgiving as gravy carriers.

SERVES 4

4 pounds potatoes,
    peeled and diced
3 tablespoons extra virgin
    olive oil
about 1⅓ cups hot milk

fresh nutmeg, grated
salt and ground black
    pepper
a few leaves fresh basil or
    sprigs fresh parsley,
    chopped

Boil the potatoes until just tender and not too mushy. Drain very well. Press the potatoes through a potato "ricer" or mash them well with a potato masher (above left). Do not pass them through a food processor or you will have a gluey mess.

Beat the olive oil into the potato and mix in just enough hot milk to make a smooth, thick purée (above right). Flavor to taste with the nutmeg and seasoning, then stir in the fresh chopped herbs. Spoon into a warm serving dish and serve as soon as possible.

COOK'S TIP

Choosing the right potato makes all the difference to mashed potatoes. A waxy variety won't be light and fluffy, and a potato which breaks down too quickly will become a slurry when mashed. In general, red potatoes will make a good mash, as will Florida Creamers and Yukon Golds.

CANDIED SWEET POTATOES

Thanksgiving dinner must include sweet potatoes. This sliced and layered version
is lightly glazed with maple syrup. Dot it with marshmallows if you like.

SERVES 8

3 pounds sweet potatoes,
  peeled
3 tablespoons butter or
  margarine

½ cup maple syrup
¾ teaspoon ground
  ginger
1 tablespoon fresh lemon
  juice

Preheat the oven to 375°F. Grease a large shallow baking dish.

Cut the potatoes in ½-inch slices. Cook them in boiling water for 10 minutes. Drain. Let cool.

Melt the butter or margarine in a small saucepan over medium heat (below left). Stir in the maple syrup until well combined. Stir in the ginger. Simmer 1 minute, then add the lemon juice.

Arrange the potato slices in one layer in the prepared baking dish, overlapping them slightly. Drizzle the

maple syrup mixture evenly over the potatoes (left). Bake until the potatoes are tender and glazed, 30–35 minutes, spooning the cooking liquid over them once or twice while they are baking.

BAKED ONIONS WITH SUN-DRIED TOMATOES

These Mediterranean-flavored baked onions are a tasty and colorful twist on the traditional creamed onions. If there are any leftovers reheat them the next day with a slice of feta cheese melted over for a delicious lunch.

SERVES 8

2 pounds pearl onions, peeled

3 teaspoons chopped fresh rosemary or ¾ teaspoon dried rosemary

4 garlic cloves, chopped

2 tablespoons chopped

fresh parsley

salt and freshly ground black pepper

1 cup sun-dried tomatoes packed in oil, drained and chopped

¾ cup olive oil

2 tablespoons white wine vinegar

baking dish.

Combine the rosemary, garlic, parsley, salt and pepper and sprinkle over the onions (right). Scatter the tomatoes over the onions. Drizzle the olive oil and vinegar on top.

Cover with a sheet of foil and bake 45 minutes, lifting the foil to baste the onions occasionally. Remove the foil and bake until the onions are golden, about 15 minutes longer (below).

Preheat the oven to 300°F. Grease a shallow baking dish.

Drop the onions into a pan of boiling water and cook 5 minutes. Drain in a colander (above left). Spread the onions in the bottom of the prepared

LONG GRAIN AND WILD RICE RING

This colorful rice ring is the essence of fall. It conjures up flocks of Canada geese
(who love it as much as we do) and the windy marshes where it grows.

SERVES 8
2 tablespoons corn oil
1 large onion, chopped
2 cups processed mixed
   long-grain and wild rice
5 cups chicken stock

½ cup dried currants
salt
6 scallions, cut diagonally
   into ¼-inch pieces
parsley sprigs, for
   garnishing

Oil a 7-cup ring mold. Set aside. Heat the oil in a large saucepan. Add the onion and soften for 5 minutes (above left). Add the rice to the pan and stir well to coat with the oil.

Stir in the chicken stock (above right) and bring to a boil. Reduce the heat to low. Stir the currants into the rice mixture. Add salt to taste. Cover and simmer until the rice is tender and the stock has been absorbed, about 20 minutes or more.

Drain the rice if necessary and transfer it to a mixing bowl. Stir in the scallions.

Pack the rice mixture into the prepared mold. Unmold it carefully onto a warmed serving platter. If you like, put parsley sprigs into the center of the ring before serving.

Zucchini and Carrot Ribbons with Brie, Black Pepper and Parsley

This recipe produces a delicious vegetarian meal, or simply a new way of presenting colorful vegetables as an accompaniment to a main course.

SERVES 4
1 large green bell pepper, diced
1 tablespoon sunflower oil
8 ounces Brie cheese
2 tablespoons crème fraîche or yogurt
1 teaspoon lemon juice
4 tablespoons milk
2 teaspoons freshly ground black pepper
2 tablespoons parsley, very finely chopped, plus extra to garnish
salt and pepper
6 large carrots
6 large zucchini

Sauté the green pepper in the sunflower oil until just tender. Place the remaining ingredients, apart from the carrots and zucchini, in a food processor and blend well. Place the mixture in a saucepan and add the green pepper to the pan (above).

Peel the carrots. Use a potato peeler to slice them into long, thin strips. Do the same thing with the zucchini. Put the carrots and zucchini in separate saucepans, add just enough water to cover, then simmer for 3 minutes until barely cooked.

Heat the sauce and pour into a shallow vegetable dish. Toss the carrot and zucchini strips together and arrange them in the sauce. Garnish with a little finely chopped parsley.

ROSEMARY BREAD

If you make two loaves of this tasty bread you might have some left for a delicious lunch
of turkey sandwiches the next day.

SERVES 4

1 × ¼ ounce package
    dried fast-action yeast
1½ cups whole wheat
    flour
1½ cups self-rising flour
2 tablespoons butter,
    plus more to grease
    bowl and pan
¼ cup warm water
    (110°F)
1 cup milk, whole or 2%
    (room temperature)

1 tablespoon sugar
1 teaspoon salt
1 tablespoon sesame
    seeds
1 tablespoon dried
    chopped onion
1 tablespoon fresh
    rosemary leaves, plus
    more to decorate
1 cup cubed Cheddar
    cheese
coarse salt, to decorate

Place the dough into a clean bowl greased with a little butter, turning it so that it becomes greased on all sides. Cover with a clean, dry cloth. Put the greased bowl and dough in a warm place for about 1½ hours, or until the dough has risen and doubled in size.

Grease a 9 × 5 inch loaf pan with the remaining butter. Knock down the dough to remove some of the air, and shape it into a loaf. Put the loaf into the pan, cover with the cloth and leave for about 1 hour until doubled in size. Preheat the oven to 375°F.

Bake for 30 minutes. During the last 5–10 minutes of baking, cover the loaf with foil to prevent it from becoming too dark. Remove from the loaf pan and leave to cool on a wire rack. Decorate with rosemary leaves and coarse salt scattered on top.

Mix the fast-action yeast with the flours in a large mixing bowl (right). Melt the butter. Stir in the warm water, milk, sugar, butter, salt, sesame seeds, onion and rosemary. Knead in the bowl thoroughly until the dough is quite smooth.

Flatten the dough, then add the cheese cubes. Quickly knead them in until they have been well combined.

TO FINISH

The great Thanksgiving feast is not over even when the turkey and all the delicious vegetable dishes have been eaten. To come is dessert and there is only one word that defines this dessert: pie. Pumpkin and apple are the classics, but other versions flavored with lemon, nuts and pears make delicious additions to the lineup. If you want to gild the lily serve hard sauce, whipped cream, flavored ice creams or frozen yogurt on the side. The important thing is to serve more than one pie so everyone can say "I think I'll just have a TINY slice of each." And tomorrow you don't have to eat very much.

PUMPKIN PIE

Here is a robustly spiced version of the Thanksgiving classic, with some chopped pecans for texture. Add two tablespoons of rum, bourbon or applejack and render this pie celestial.

SERVES 8

1½ cups cooked or
  canned pumpkin
2 cups light cream
⅔ cup light brown sugar,
  firmly packed
¼ teaspoon salt
1 teaspoon ground
  cinnamon
½ teaspoon ground
  ginger
¼ teaspoon ground
  cloves

⅛ teaspoon grated
  nutmeg
2 eggs

For the crust
1⅓ cups flour
½ teaspoon salt
½ cup shortening
2–3 tablespoons ice water
¼ cup pecans, chopped

Preheat the oven to 425°F.

To make the crust, sift the flour and salt into a mixing bowl. Using a pastry blender (left), cut in the shortening until the mixture resembles coarse crumbs. Sprinkle in the water, 1 tablespoon at a time. Toss lightly with your fingers or a fork until the dough will form a ball.

On a lightly floured surface, roll out the dough to ¼-inch thickness. Use it to line a 9-inch pie pan (above left), easing the dough in and being careful not to stretch it. Trim off the excess dough.

Use the dough trimmings to make a decorative rope edge. Cut in strips and twist together in pairs (above right). Dampen the rim of the pie shell and press on the rope edge. Or make a fluted edge. Sprinkle the chopped pecans over the bottom of the pie shell.

With a whisk or an electric mixer on medium speed, beat together the pumpkin, cream, brown sugar, salt, spices, and eggs.

Pour the pumpkin mixture into the pie shell. Bake 10 minutes, then reduce the heat to 350°F and continue baking until the filling is set, about 45 minutes. Let the pie cool in the pan, set on a wire rack.

MAPLE WALNUT PIE

The tastes of maple and walnut marry particularly well. Pipe an edge of whipped cream
around the top for visual and gastronomic perfection.

SERVES 8
3 eggs
1/8 teaspoon salt
1/4 cup granulated sugar
4 tablespoons butter or
  margarine, melted
1 cup pure maple syrup
1 cup walnuts, chopped
whipped cream, for
  decorating

For the crust
1/2 cup all-purpose flour
1/2 cup whole wheat flour
1/8 teaspoon salt
4 tablespoons cold butter,
  cut in pieces
3 tablespoons cold
  shortening, cut in pieces
1 egg yolk
2–3 tablespoons ice water

For the crust, mix the flours and salt in a bowl. Add the butter and shortening and cut in with a pastry blender until the mixture resembles coarse crumbs. With a fork, stir in the egg yolk and just enough water to bind the dough. Gather into a ball, wrap in wax paper, and refrigerate for 20 minutes.

Preheat the oven to 425°F. Then on a lightly floured surface, roll out the dough to 1/8 inch thick and line a 9-inch pie pan. Trim the edge. To decorate, with a small heart-shaped cutter, stamp out enough hearts to go around the rim of the pie. Brush the edge with water, then arrange the dough hearts all around.

Prick the bottom with a fork. Line with crumpled wax paper and fill with pie weights. Bake 10 minutes.

Remove the paper and weights and continue baking until golden brown, 3–6 minutes more.

In a bowl, whisk the eggs, salt, and sugar together. Stir in the butter and maple syrup.

Set the pie shell on a baking sheet. Pour in the filling, then sprinkle over the nuts. Bake until just set, about 35 minutes. Cool on a rack. Decorate with cream.

LEMON ALMOND TART

This is a light and elegant continental cousin to its sturdier American counterpart.
Its tangy flavor will tempt the most sated holiday diners.

SERVES 8
¾ cup blanched almonds
½ cup sugar
2 eggs
grated rind and juice of
  1½ lemons
½ cup (1 stick) butter,
  melted
strips of lemon rind, for
  decorating

For the crust
1¼ cups flour
1 tablespoon sugar
½ teaspoon salt
½ teaspoon baking
  powder
6 tablespoons cold
  unsalted butter, cut
  in pieces
3–4 tablespoons
  whipping cream

For the crust, sift the flour, sugar, salt, and baking powder into a bowl. Add the butter and cut in with a pastry blender until the mixture resembles coarse crumbs. With a fork, stir in just enough cream to bind the dough.

Gather into a ball and transfer to a lightly floured surface. Roll out the dough about ⅛ inch thick and transfer to a 9-inch tart pan. Trim the edge. Prick the base with a fork and refrigerate for 20 minutes.

Set a baking sheet in the oven. Preheat to 400°F. Line the tart shell with crumpled wax paper and fill with pie weights. Bake for 12 minutes. Remove the paper and weights and continue baking until golden,

6–8 minutes more. Reduce the oven to 350°F.

Grind the almonds with 1 tablespoon of the sugar. Set a mixing bowl over a pan of hot water. Add the eggs and the remaining sugar, and beat with an electric mixer until the mixture is thick and pale. Stir in the lemon rind and juice, butter, and ground almonds. Pour into the prebaked shell. Bake until golden and set, about 35 minutes. Decorate with lemon rind.

A-One Apple Pie

~

Although apple pie tastes wonderful all year round, it is especially good in the fall
when apples are freshly picked. Serve a sharp Cheddar cheese alongside the pie.

SERVES 4

6 cups peeled and sliced
  tart apples, such as
  Granny Smith or
  MacIntosh (about
  2 pounds)
1 tablespoon fresh lemon
  juice
1 teaspoon vanilla extract
½ cup sugar
½ teaspoon ground
  cinnamon
1½ tablespoons butter
  or margarine

1 egg yolk
2 teaspoons whipping
  cream

For the crust
2 cups flour
1 teaspoon salt
¾ cup shortening
4–5 tablespoons ice water
1 tablespoon quick-
  cooking tapioca

Preheat the oven to 450°F.
To make the crust, sift the flour and salt into a
mixing bowl. Using a pastry blender, cut in the
shortening until the mixture resembles coarse crumbs.

Sprinkle in the water, 1 tablespoon at a time, tossing
lightly with your fingertips or with a fork until the
dough will form a ball.

Divide the dough in half and shape each half into a
ball. On a lightly floured surface, roll out one of the
balls to a circle about 12 inches in diameter.

Use it to line a 9-inch pie pan, easing the dough in
and being careful not to stretch it. Trim off the excess
dough and use the trimmings for decorating. Sprinkle
the tapioca over the bottom of the pie shell.

Roll out the remaining dough to ⅛-inch thickness.
Cut out 8 large leaf-shapes (above left) and cut the
trimmings into small leaf shapes. Score the leaves with
the back of the knife to mark veins.

In a bowl, toss the apples with the lemon juice,
vanilla, sugar, and cinnamon. Fill the pie shell with the
apple mixture and dot with the butter or margarine.
Arrange the large pastry leaves in a decorative pattern
on top. Decorate the edge with small leaves (above
right). Mix the egg yolk and cream and brush over the
leaves to glaze them. Bake for about 10 minutes, then
reduce the heat to 350°F and bake until the pastry is
golden, 35–45 minutes.

Pear and Hazelnut Flan

Though canned pears work well in this recipe, use fresh ones and poach them yourself
if you can. Just simmer 4 peeled pears in sugar water until tender, then core and half them
and place them on the pie filling.

Serves 4
1 cup flour
¾ cup whole wheat flour
8 tablespoons sunflower
  margarine
3 tablespoons cold water

Filling
½ cup self-rising flour
1 cup ground hazelnuts
1 teaspoon vanilla extract

2 ounces superfine sugar
4 tablespoons butter,
  softened
2 eggs, beaten
3 tablespoons raspberry
  jam
1 × 14 ounce can pears
  in natural juice
a few chopped hazelnuts,
  to decorate

Stir the flours well in a large mixing bowl, then rub in the margarine until it resembles fine crumbs. Mix to a firm dough with the water.

Roll out the pastry and line a 9–10-inch pie pan, pressing it firmly up the sides after trimming, so the pastry sits above the pan (above). Prick the base, line with waxed paper and fill with pie weights. Chill for 30 minutes.

Preheat the oven to 400°F. Place the pie pan on a baking sheet and bake for 20 minutes, removing the paper and weights for the last 5.

Meanwhile, beat all the filling ingredients together except for the jam and pears (above left). If the mixture is a little thick, stir in some pear juice.

Reduce the oven temperature to 350°F. Spread the jam on the pastry then spoon in the filling (below left).

Drain the pears and arrange cut side down in the filling (below right). Scatter over the nuts and bake for 30 minutes until risen, firm and golden brown.

PLUM PIE

Little Jack Horner would love this sweet/tart pie, with a scoop of vanilla ice cream.

SERVES 4

2 pounds red or purple
  plums
grated rind of 1 lemon
1 tablespoon fresh lemon
  juice
½–¾ cup sugar
3 tablespoons quick-
  cooking tapioca
⅛ teaspoon salt
½ teaspoon ground
  cinnamon

¼ teaspoon grated
  nutmeg

For the crust
2 cups flour
1 teaspoon salt
6 tablespoons cold butter,
  cut in pieces
4 tablespoons cold
  shortening, cut in pieces
¼–½ cup ice water
milk, for glazing

For the crust, sift the flour and salt into a bowl. Add the butter and shortening and cut in with a pastry blender until the mixture resembles coarse crumbs. Stir in just enough water to bind the dough. Gather into 2 balls, one slightly larger than the other. Wrap and refrigerate for 20 minutes.

Place a baking sheet in the center of the oven and preheat to 425°F. On a lightly floured surface, roll out the larger dough ball about ⅛ inch thick. Transfer to a 9-inch pie pan and trim the edge.

Halve the plums, discard the pits, and cut in large pieces. Mix all the filling ingredients together (if the plums are tart, use ¾ cup sugar). Fill the pie shell.

Roll out the remaining dough and place on a baking tray lined with wax paper. Stamp out 4 heart shapes. Transfer them to the pie using the wax paper.

Trim to leave a ¾-inch overhang. Fold the top edge under the bottom and pinch to seal. Arrange the dough hearts on top. Brush with the milk. Bake for 15 minutes. Reduce the heat to 350°F and bake 30–35 minutes more. If the crust browns too quickly, protect with a sheet of foil.

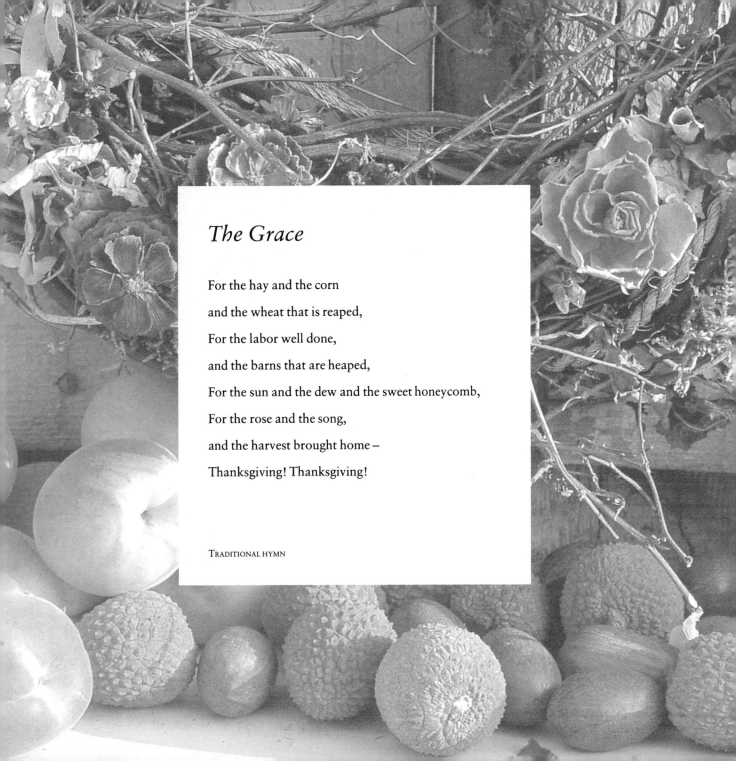

The Grace

For the hay and the corn

and the wheat that is reaped,

For the labor well done,

and the barns that are heaped,

For the sun and the dew and the sweet honeycomb,

For the rose and the song,

and the harvest brought home –

Thanksgiving! Thanksgiving!

TRADITIONAL HYMN

INDEX

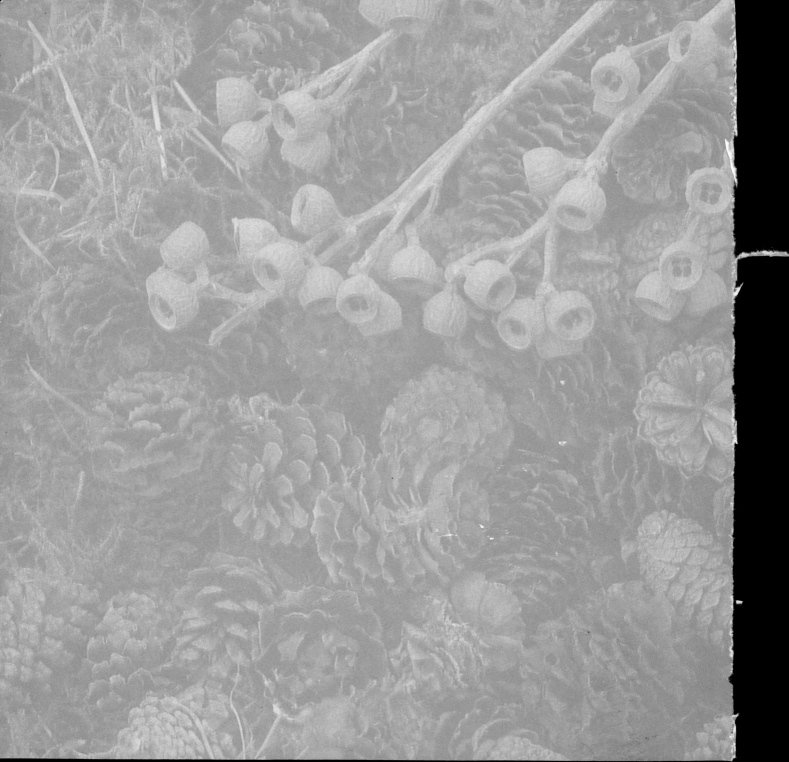